SCENES FROM
Columbia's Riverbanks
A HISTORY OF THE WATERWAYS

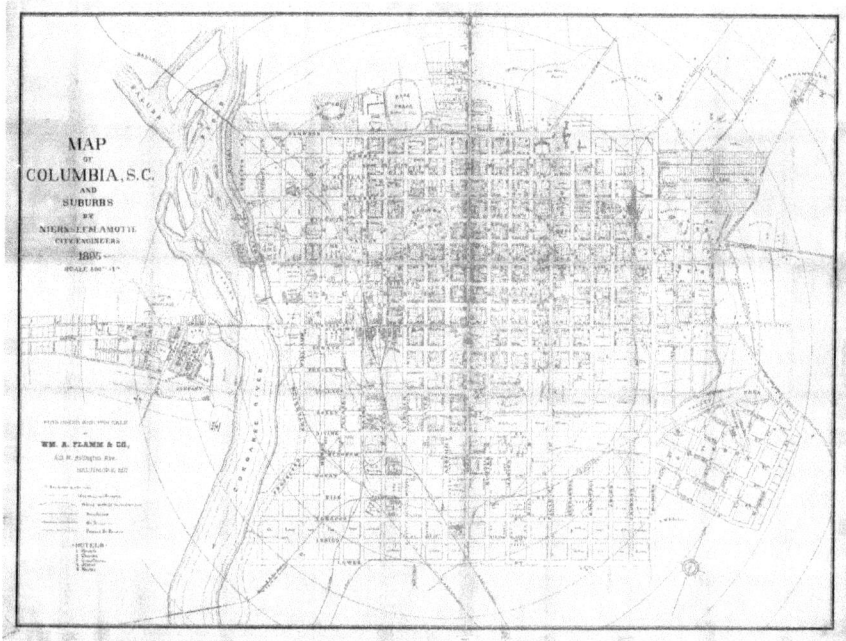

An 1895 map of Columbia and its rivers. *Courtesy of the South Caroliniana Library, University of South Carolina.*

S CENES FROM

Columbia's Riverbanks

A HISTORY OF THE WATERWAYS

Vennie Deas-Moore

With a Foreword by Fritz Hamer
South Carolina State Museum

The
History
PRESS

Published by The History Press
Charleston, SC 29403
www.historypress.net

Copyright © 2008 by Vennie Deas-Moore
All rights reserved.
All photographs by the author unless otherwise noted.

First published 2008

ISBN 978.1.54023.429.2

Library of Congress Cataloging-in-Publication Data

Deas-Moore, Vennie.
Scenes from Columbia's riverbanks : a history of the waterways / Vennie
Deas-Moore.
p. cm.
ISBN-13: 978.1.54023.429.2

1. Columbia (S.C.)--History. 2. Columbia (S.C.)--Pictorial works. 3.
Rivers--South Carolina--Columbia--History. 4. Rivers--South
Carolina--Columbia--Pictorial works. 5. Broad River (N.C. and
S.C.)--History. 6. Broad River (N.C. and S.C.)--Pictorial works. 7.
Congaree River (S.C.)--History. 8. Congaree River (S.C.)--Pictorial works.
9. Saluda River (S.C.)--History. 10. Saluda River (S.C.)--Pictorial works.
11. Landscape--South Carolina--Columbia--Pictorial works. I. Title.
F279.C7M675 2008
975.7'71001693--dc22
2007046016

*To my children: Keith, Derek and daughter-in-law Carlene
for their love of the outdoors.*

CONTENTS

FOREWORD

S outh Carolina is full of fascinating stories—some well known and others still to be discovered. Whether they focus on the lives of the generations of families who toiled in rice and cotton fields or those who struggled to make a living in the burgeoning textile mills that began to dot the upper parts of the state by the late nineteenth century, these stories show the enduring spirit and energy of South Carolinians from many different walks of life. And all of these walks of life are connected to the varied landscapes with which South Carolina is blessed.

To discover and chronicle the innumerable stories and landscapes of this state takes a different, equally dedicated kind of endurance and spirit. Energy and patience are essential in digging through archives, interviewing people and following leads gleaned from each of these processes. Thankfully, there are individuals in our state who have these qualities. Vennie Deas-Moore is one of them. For years she has dug persistently into the records of the South Carolina Department of Archives and History, the South Caroliniana

Library, the South Carolina Historical Society and many other lesser known places in search of written accounts, photographs and official records to document the lives of the people and the landscapes across the Palmetto State. She has also carried a camera with her to virtually every corner of the state to chronicle its varied landscapes and the historic remnants that still exist in many areas. She has authored two books so that people can learn from her vast research and the photographs she has taken. These books are not only important for the public today, but they will also serve future generations as they seek to learn about how these land areas appeared in the beginning of the twenty-first century.

Now Vennie has produced her third book, focusing on the landscapes along the Midland's rivers and canals. Using her camera and a few images taken by other photographers, she documents the current landscapes of these waterways and their banks. Once an essential transportation route for Upcountry farmers and their agricultural products to Lowcountry ports, in recent years this geographical zone has become an important recreational area in the Midlands. It provides for many citizens an area to exercise and an inner city link to the natural world—particularly through the expanding riverwalk with miles of trails on both sides of the river. As readers review these images and the brief narrative, they may also gain a glimpse of the important history of this region and discover the historic remnants that can be found amidst the expanding wilderness that has returned to this once important industrial area.

As Vennie follows the rivers, the reader will see how they have become centers for recreation—whether fishing, visiting the Riverbanks Zoo and its Botanical Gardens located near the remains of an old textile mill or the homeless using a bridge for shelter. Although today the emphasis on these rivers and banks is for recreation and preserving the natural environment, some organizations still make their livings near these waterways. This is particularly the case for the rock quarry that remains active near the Congaree. And soon the University of South Carolina will be creating research labs and a ballpark near the east bank of the same river to remake the landscape once again.

As you read Vennie's narrative and examine the many photographs she has taken documenting the riverbanks, you will discover the rich natural landscapes and gain a glimpse of the rich history of this part of South Carolina. I hope that this study will help you to appreciate a natural landscape that, until recently, has been largely overlooked—if not neglected.

Fritz Hamer
South Carolina State Museum
October 2007

ACKNOWLEDGEMENTS

M any people deserve my gratitude for their help in this project. Thank you to Lynn Robertson of the McKissick Museum and Fritz Hamer of the South Carolina State Museum for their support throughout this project. Columbia Regional Visitors Center suggested that I explore the riverbanks, which led me to embark on this project. The local history room at the Richland County Public Library, the South Caroliniana Library at the University of South Carolina, John Hammond Moore and Greater Columbia Civil War Alliance were all essential resources. Lee Handford and the rest of the staff at The History Press have also been a great help. Thanks to Keith Moore and Clara Green for financial support, and to the CVS Pharmacy Photo Lab for downloading over a thousand images.

INTRODUCTION

*Columbia owes its existence to the fact that it was
located at the head of navigation on large rivers,
giving it access to the outside world, and it possessed a
supporting tributary area around and behind it.*
—Samuel M. Derrick

As South Carolina expanded inland, the rivers of the
Lowcountry provided transportation into the fall lines
where the shoals and rapids occurred along the Congaree,
Saluda and Broad Rivers. This flood plain environment was
an area of swamps bordered by diverse hardwood bluffs that
was subject to seasonal flooding.

In the early 1700s, Fort Congaree—a backcountry fort—
was built along the bend of Congaree Creek. A nearby
Native American trading post was a point of exchange for
goods. Serving as a trading area, settlement, frontier outpost
and military staging point, Fort Congaree was a crossroads
of the great trading paths of the Catawba and Cherokee
Nations and a center of backcountry development.

Above the Congaree, it was no man's land—although both the Catawba and the Cherokee traveled the riverbanks to fish and hunt. The Broad River was known as *Eswa Huppiday*, meaning "Line River." The Catawba laid claim to the north of the Broad River, and the Cherokee hunted on the southern side of the river.

Small farmers moved into the backcountry of South Carolina to find fertile farmland. This created "buffer zones" between the backcountry and the heavy coastal settlements. Early settlers entered this area, displacing the Native Americans. The Native American population declined rapidly due to smallpox epidemics brought to the New World by European settlers. Wealthy planters moved into the Congaree River valley and introduced the plantation system to the region. Utilizing old Native American trading paths, settlers built roads and ferries across the swamp to provide a means of transporting produce and livestock to markets on the coast—namely, to Charleston.

In 1753, the village of Granby was laid out. Granby was made the county seat of government. A courthouse, jail, stores, a boat landing and numerous homes were built. Martin Friday's ferry was built close to the town and was a major ferry crossing along the Congaree River. In 1771, Wade Hampton built a bridge across the Congaree, connecting Columbia to Granby.

It was 1786 when the South Carolina General Assembly directed that the seat of state government be moved from

Charleston to Columbia. The infant town of Columbia was a plateau 350 feet above sea level, overlooking the Congaree River at the confluence of the Broad and Saluda Rivers. Lower-lying Granby was all but forgotten. Hampton's bridge was destroyed by a freshet. A second bridge was built, but it too was destroyed in 1796. For some years, ferryboats were the only means of crossing the streams.

As river traffic increased, it became necessary to build a canal. The canal was completed in 1824. It had an eight-foot-wide towpath on each side. The canal had four lifting water transport locks and one guard lock for the thirty-four-foot descent of the river. The canal was excavated below the falls on the Broad River, just north of Columbia. The Columbia Canal was a notable example of the engineering expertise of the nineteenth century. Robert Mills, a federal architect, was instrumental in the development of the canal. It was part of the state-sponsored system of internal improvements designed to create inexpensive and efficient transportation facilities across South Carolina. It played an important role in the commercial and industrial development of Columbia.

The Congaree River was navigable for steamboats from the southwest end of Columbia to the Santee River—a total waterway of more than 175 miles in length that drained into the Atlantic Ocean. For many years the waterway was the highway. Steamboats, tugs and canal boats traveled regularly from Columbia's rivers to the Santee Canal, transporting

A downstream view of a diversion dam canal—north to south, with a canal lock. *Courtesy of South Carolina Department of Archives and History.*

more than thirty thousand bales of cotton from Columbia to Charleston annually, with full return freights. For a time, there was a landing at Granby, and steamboats plied between Columbia and Charleston Harbor. In 1822, the *Carolina* made the trip upriver in four and a half days and loaded nine hundred bales of cotton on towboats.

Another era of industry burgeoned along the rivers and spread into the city of Columbia proper. Some fifty-seven commercial, warehouse and light industrial properties were developed within Columbia's borders. The beginning of the

Detailed gate controls—
looking east. *Courtesy of South
Carolina Department of Archives
and History.*

development was in the area along Gervais Street in the city's
principal western artery.

The ferryboat was used until 1827, at which time the
Columbia Bridge Company constructed a bridge across the
river at the foot of Gervais Street. The Broad River Bridge was
built two years later in 1829. A fifteen-hundred-foot dam was
constructed on the Broad River near its confluence with the
Saluda River to channel the water into the Columbia Canal.

The Saluda Factory, built around 1830, was among the
first textile firms in the state, and as such it was opposed by

19

A general view of the floodgate structure—top of canal, east to west.
Courtesy of South Carolina Department of Archives and History.

a number of influential South Carolinians who preferred a
wealthy agrarian society.

In 1840, the State of South Carolina dropped its subsidy
of the canal. In 1842, the railroads came to Columbia and
the traffic on the canal decreased. At that time, the primary
use of the canal transferred to local commerce and it began
to provide hydraulic power for industries. The Columbia
Canal was the only canal project in the state that remained
in use after the advent of the railroad.

A diversion dam. The dam channeled water into the Columbia Canal.
Courtesy of South Carolina Department of Archives and History.

In 1846 the South Carolina Railroad Depot came to Columbia. The railroad services went to the western area of the state—to Greenville, Anderson and Spartanburg.

The waterworks system became a municipal enterprise. The first plant was developed in what is now Finley Park. The water was secured from two springs and pumped up to Arsenal Hill. Sometime after 1855, when a hundred-thousand-dollar bond was issued for new waterworks, a new plant was fed with spring water until the pumping station could be moved across the canal and water from the river used. The great falls of the Congaree begin at the upper end of Columbia and terminate a little below the lower end of town. Robert Mill described the water plant as follows:

> *Columbia is amply supplied with spring water which is forced up by a steam power 120 feet from springs issuing from a valley between the town and river. It is distributed through the principal streets in cast iron pipes and then conveyed from these main conduits in leaden pipes.*

It was on February 17, 1865, when General W.T. Sherman's army entered the city and fires almost destroyed Columbia.

A historic photograph of water spilling over a dam at the water power plant. *Courtesy of the South Carolina Department of Archives and History.*

The Confederate troops retreated, and Mayor Thomas J. Goodwyn surrendered the city of Columbia on that same day. The following was published in *Harper's Weekly*:

> *The bridge had been burnt by Wheeler's men the night before we arrived and the 30th Ohio (Col. Theodore Jones Brigade 2nd Division) crossed in a flat boat and skirmished with the enemy driving them to the Broad River.*

Sherman must have looked across the Congaree River from what is now Guignard Park. Below him were the smoldering ruins of bridges. The wooden bridge built across the Congaree River was burned to delay Sherman's army. They then traveled toward the Broad River Bridge—it was also burned. Using a rope extended across the river, the Northern troops pulled themselves to the other side on a pontoon boat.

General Howard of Sherman's army set fire to the Saluda Factory and left it in ruins. After driving off Rebel sharpshooters hidden in the rocks of what is now Riverbanks Zoo, Howard's men built a pontoon bridge, crossed the river and camped on the peninsula between the Saluda and Broad Rivers (near the current intersection of Greystone Boulevard and Interstate 126).

After the Civil War, the Saluda Factory was rebuilt as a three-story wooden structure on the original granite foundation. An accidental fire on August 2, 1884, destroyed the factory for a second time and it was never rebuilt.

Columbia was greatly changed by the Civil War. Like a phoenix, Columbia made an effort to rise from the ashes and industrialized. Those in power decided to enlarge the canal as a means of providing a power source to aid in the industrial development of Columbia. This was completed in 1888.

The revised design started at Gervais Street and extended about three and a half miles north along the Congaree and Broad Rivers. It included a new diversion dam, an entry lock and a waste weir. In 1891 the canal extended upstream of Bull Sluice. It ran along the Congaree for about three miles and ended across from Granby Landing. Electricity was generated from the Columbia Canal. The need for electrical power increased, and in response the Broad River Power Company built the dam on the Broad River.

In 1894, Arethas Blood, president of Columbia Mills Company, started the motors in the new Columbia Duck Mill. This marked the first time that a textile mill was operated by electrical power to produce heavy cotton duck material.

As a result of the mill growth, mill villages were being developed along the riverbanks. The town of Brookland— named because of the vast number of clear-water brooks throughout the area—emerged as a planned residential community for workers at the Columbia Duck Mill. The mill was situated on the eastern shore of the Congaree and the working population lived on the western shore. The

The floodgate controls to a diversion dam—east to west view. *Courtesy of South Carolina Department of Archives and History.*

community's original name persisted until 1938 when the town name was changed to West Columbia.

A major problem the city faced was how to transport the workers across the Congaree to their job sites. At first ferryboats were used for this purpose, but as the working population increased and the demand of more people wanting to visit Columbia rose, this soon became impractical. The Guignard family built a bridge across the Congaree River. Made of wood, it provided not only access to the mill, but also eased transportation of both people and freight.

A view of the Columbia Canal Hydroelectric Plant, canal and water gates—southwest side, looking west. The plant was built at the southern end of the canal and produced power for industry, the city of Columbia and the street railway system. It is still operated by the South Carolina Gas & Electric Co. *Courtesy of the Library of Congress.*

Six other textile mills were built in Columbia between 1890 and 1905. During this period, the cotton textile industry in South Carolina experienced remarkable growth. Cotton production in the state was among the largest in the country.

The Granby Mill and adjacent Granby Mill Village were designed, built and managed by the prominent textile mill designer W.B. Smith Whaley, whose firm was one of the

The Columbia Canal Hydroelectric Plant was designed to supply electricity to the Columbia Mills. This was one of the first powerhouses in the nation to utilize hydroelectric power to drive a large textile mill. The area also contained the city's gas works, built circa 1869; the first electric light plant, built circa 1891; and the street railway company barn, built circa 1886. *Courtesy of South Carolina Department of Archives and History.*

Southeast's most prolific and innovative. Granby, initially constructed in 1896–97, was the second Columbia mill built by Whaley; the first was the Richland Mill in 1894–95. Granby represented Whaley's first major technological improvement in mill design. It was the first cotton mill in the state to be powered by a remote, off-site source of hydroelectric power. The Granby Mill Village depicts some of the most well-preserved turn-of-the-century mill village saltboxes found in the state, with 112 of the 121 original dwellings remaining—most retain a high degree of physical integrity.

Olympia Mills was one of the largest cotton mills in the world operating under one roof—it had 110,000 spindles.

Columbia lies on a large outcrop of granite. It was not until the 1850s that any attempt was made to use this durable building material. Work on the state penitentiary on the Congaree River began during the administration of Governor Orr in 1867—the granite used was quarried from the bed of the Broad River.

A quarry was opened on the river behind Granby Mill Village. There were large deposits of rich calcium marls that could easily be hauled by rail and truck to the Congaree River. Additionally, there were numerous limestone and granite deposits—some of the latter were of an exceedingly high grade known as monumental granite. Sand in endless qualities was blasted. Today materials are quarried for highway building, and immense clay and shale deposits furnish raw material for brick and shale plants.

The statehouse was the first structure in the city made of this stone. The stone was of excellent quality and the great monolithic columns on the front and back porches testify to its fine grain and beauty. In order to carry the stone from the quarry to the site of the statehouse, a tram road was built that ran from the quarry to the back of the building. The immense stones, weighing tons, were put on the trams and hauled up the hill by oxen to the building where they were sawed, dressed and carved.

Mining operations at the quarry have been in almost continuous existence since 1850, and the quarry itself has been in operation since 1916. Basically a family affair, Palmetto Quarries, Inc., was headed by President Lott; his son, George D.J., vice-president; Hamilton Lott, chief engineer; and Sam Dreyfuss, sales manager. Now it is the Vulcan Materials Company.

The Guignard Brick Works produced bricks for many buildings constructed in Columbia and throughout South Carolina from around 1900 through the mid-twentieth century. The brick works evolved throughout more than a hundred years of operation at this site in a process in which the fuels and methods for firing brick changed from wood to coal to gas.

The Richland Distilling Company of Columbia was built and put into operation in 1901 for the purpose of supplying liquor to the South Carolina Dispensary. The Dispensary also spawned the creation of several other businesses like the Carolina Glass Company. The distillery was located on the Congaree River between the Olympia Mill Village and the river. Richland Distilling was owned and operated by a corporation chartered under the laws of South Carolina. The distillery was a very large complex of buildings and rooms in which specific activities of distilling occurred.

After the abolition of the South Carolina Dispensary in 1907, the Richland Distilling Company went out of business and into bankruptcy. The equipment was sold for salvage and the land and building were sold for taxes. Only the base of the vats in the ground and the brick ruins remain of this once bustling complex. Today this site sits along the Three Rivers Greenway near Granby.

In the early part of the twentieth century, Irwin Park sprawled along the canal in the area of the water plant. On Sunday afternoons, the park was a place for strolling, sitting and picnicking. The canal bank was lined with trees and bushes, overshadowed by the brick wall of the penitentiary. The landscape was reminiscent of the Impressionist paintings of European parks. There was also a zoo surrounded by a heavy wire fence. In the zoo, families could observe camels, deer, ostriches and peacocks.

One of four open spandrel arch bridges of reinforced concrete in South Carolina, the Gervais Street Bridge spans the Congaree River and links Columbia to the western and southern parts of the state. At the time of its construction, which began in February 1926 and was completed in June 1928, the bridge had the widest roadway in the state. From 1928 to 1953, the Gervais Street Bridge was the only bridge in Columbia that crossed the Congaree River and is the earliest and most decorative of the three bridges that now cross the river.

The 1,415-foot reinforced concrete bridge was constructed by the Hardaway Contracting Company of Columbus, Georgia. It cost $597,167 to construct. The bridge was designed by Joseph W. Barnwell of Charleston—a bridge engineer for the state highway department. Above the flanking balustrades on the bridge are cast-iron light fixtures. The decorative fixtures have the letter *C* and a palmetto on their bases, a vine pattern on their eight-sided posts and an acanthus leaf design on their necking.

The Saluda River Valley was settled by Dutch immigrants in the 1700s. They migrated into the fork of the valley, which was appropriately given the name Dutch Fork. Scotch, Irish

One of four open spandrel arch bridges of reinforced concrete in South Carolina, the Gervais Street Bridge spans the Congaree River and links Columbia to the western and southern parts of the state. *Courtesy of the Library of Congress.*

and German immigrants also came to the area. General Robert E. Lee, then in the corps of engineers, was one of the first to recognize the potential of the Saluda River Valley. A frequently flooded area, he saw it as an ideal site for a dam. The dam would harness power for grinding corn and wheat and for powering gristmills. The goods would then be transported to and from the Lowcountry.

A palmetto and crescent moon lamp on the Gervais Street Bridge. *Courtesy of the Library of Congress.*

In 1927, a contract was awarded for the construction of the world's largest earthen dam. Water was allowed to rise in stages until it reached a maximum of 360 feet above mean sea level in 1933. Many acres of farmland, homesites, cemeteries, gristmills and ferries and many miles of roadway were inundated—most never to be seen again. It created one of the world's largest man-made lakes.

Lake Murray is some forty-one miles long, fourteen miles wide and covers seventy-eight square miles. Lake Murray extends across several counties—Lexington, Saluda, Newberry and Richland. It serves as a storage reservoir for the operation of the Saluda Hydro and cools water for the McMeekin steam-electric generating plant.

Across the Saluda Dam, there are five towers. These round landmarks are 223 feet in height. The four smaller towers provide water from the bottom of the lake into 986-foot-long penstocks. Each penstock is 16 feet in diameter and is built of steel plates sewn together with over 220,000 rivets. The largest tower feeds water to the massive arch conduct, which diverted the river during construction and afterward served as the course for an additional penstock to supply a future turbine.

Columbia has an extensive waterfront. Dams, bridges, trestles, waterworks, docks and other major structures dot the waterscape all the way from the Congaree River to the Broad River to the Saluda River, ending at Lake Murray. The waterways have been all but forgotten. As I walked these

Introduction

riverbanks over the last year, my exploration was haunted by their lively and productive pasts.

SCENES FROM

Columbia's
Riverbanks
A HISTORY OF THE WATERWAYS

A water weir.

The Saluda River at West Columbia.

The Broad River Dam.

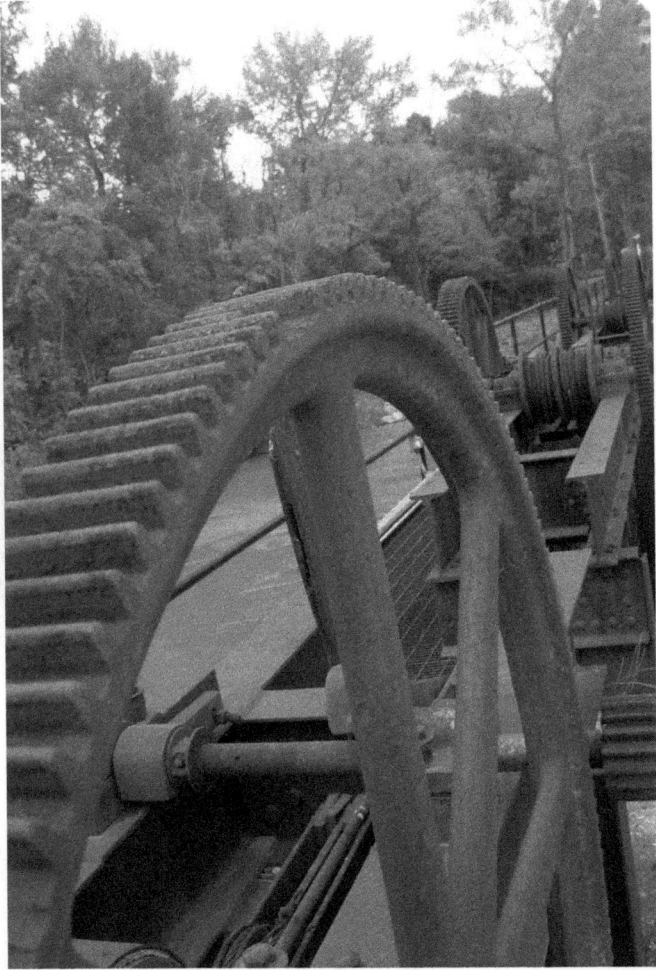

Detailed gear on the diversion dam.

A full view of the floodgate structure at the top of the canal.

A railroad trestle over the Congaree River. This railroad trestle serves both the Southern and Seaboard Railways, serving points south from Columbia.

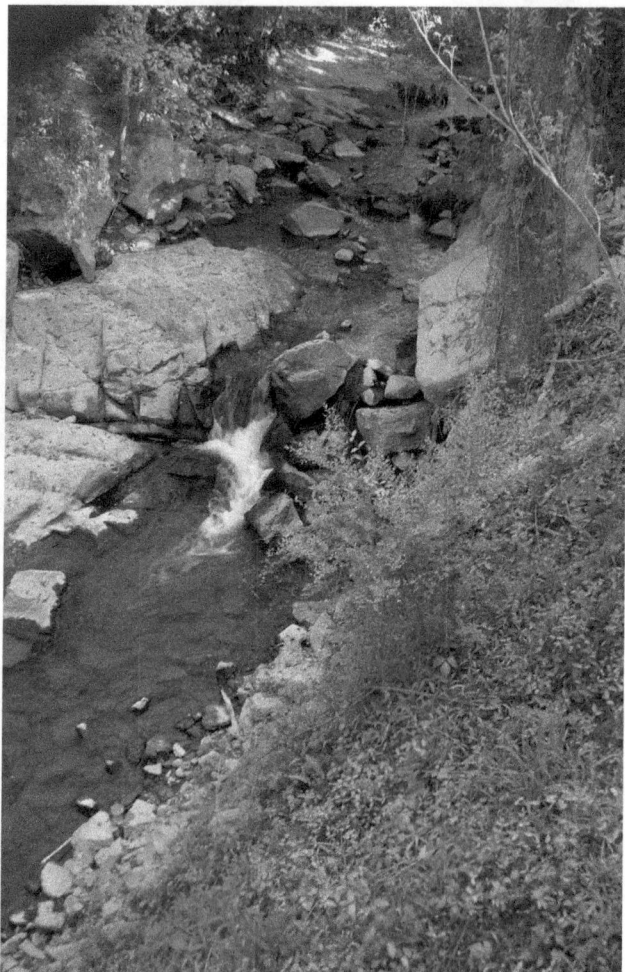

A waterfall through the rocks.

A view of the landing and locks on the Congaree River below Cayce. In early days, over sixty thousand bales of cotton were transported along the canal by two steamboats and a number of bay and canal boats. A channel to a turnaround basin was dug in the Congaree River at the foot of Gervais Street.

The Broad River Dam, near Columbia's city limits, shunts water down the Columbia Canal to waterworks at Gervais Street.

The overlook at the dam on the Broad River.

The Gervais Street Bridge, overlooking the McMillan Bridge along the Congaree River.

The Columbia Canal greatly aided the development of Columbia.

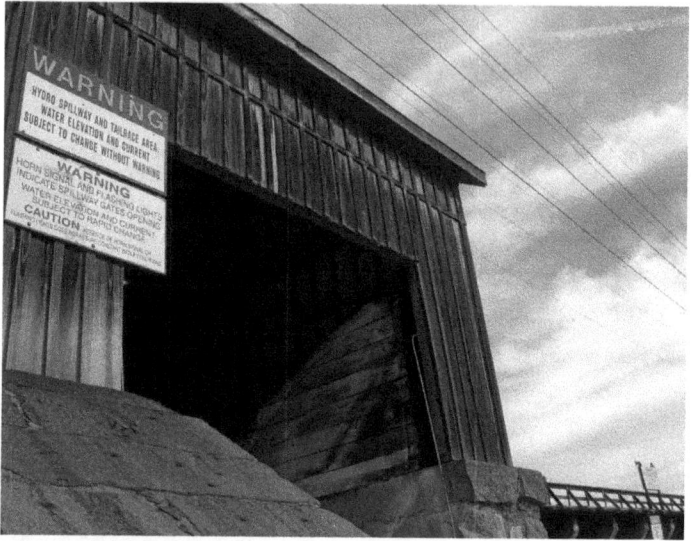

A shed over a water spill.

Rushing waters.

The Columbia Canal Hydroelectric Plant.

The South Carolina State Museum. In 1893, Mount Vernon Mill, a large, four-story factory, was located above the Congaree River. To power the alternating current motors in the mills, a powerhouse was built on the canal about six hundred feet away. The Columbia Mills building was believed to be the first textile plant in the nation to be operated by electricity. The building provided for the manufacture of cotton duck fabric. Columbia Mills became part of Mount Vernon-Woodberry Cotton Duck Company, Mount Vernon-Woodberry Mills, Inc. and finally Mount Vernon Mills, Inc. It continued to manufacture cotton duck until 1981 when the plant was closed. It is now the South Carolina State Museum (South Carolina State Archives).

This bridge was burned to stop Sherman's army from entering the city of Columbia.

The first electric light plant was built in 1891 on Gates Street between Gervais and Lady Streets. The power was taken form the canal. In 1893, electricity was being generated from the canal.

A fishing hole at the 240-acre Saluda Shoals Park.

The old prison wall faces the water plant weir.

A bridge over the canal connects the new water plant with the old water plant.

These round landmarks are intake towers standing 223 feet in height. The four smaller towers provide water for the bottom of Lake Murray's 986-foot-long penstocks. Each penstock is 16 feet in diameter and is built of steel plates.

Old kilns at the Guignard Brick Works. The Guignard brick plant manufactured building bricks and was in operation when Columbia was first established. According to the South Carolina Department of Archives and history:

> *The Guignard Brick Works complex includes four brick beehive kilns, a historic brick office and remnants of other industrial features of the brick works, and has archaeological potential. Three of the four kilns were built ca. 1919, while the fourth was built in 1932 to replace a ca. 1900 kiln which burned beyond repair. These beehive kilns, also called circular downdraft kilns, are constructed of brick, topped with brick domes, and measure approximately 18' high and 35' in diameter. A one-story hip roof brick office building, ca. 1900, stands west of the kilns. The Guignard Brick Works flourished and expanded its operations with the building boom in Columbia which began in the late 1890s and was in full swing by 1900.*

An old water plant.

The Junior Wildwater World Championship was held on the Saluda River on July 16–19, 2007.

Warning signs for the hydroelectric spillway.

The Lake Murray Marina. Lake Murray is some forty-one miles long, fourteen miles wide and covers seventy-eight square miles—or approximately fifty thousand acres. Many acres of farmland, homesites, cemeteries, gristmills and ferries and many miles of roadway were purposely flooded, never to be seen again.

The Dreher Shoals Dam at Lake Murray. In 1927, a contract was awarded for the construction of the world's largest earthen dam to be thrown across the valley of the Saluda River ten miles from Columbia. The Lexington Water Power Company was organized to construct a dam and powerhouse, and it completed the development at Lake Murray on the Saluda River in 1930. The cost of this development was $20 million. At the time of its completion, the earthen dam stood 208 feet high and stretched nearly a mile and a half long. The lake itself is 41 miles long and 14 miles wide at its widest point and contains over 760 billion gallons of water with a shoreline of over 600 miles. The high pool elevation of Lake Murray is at 360 feet above mean sea level. It is now one of the largest artificial lakes in the world for a power project, with an uninterrupted flow of 200,000 hydroelectric horsepower.

Stepping stones. The rushing water along the Congaree River is gorged with the flotsam of several miles of fallen leaves, broken branches and dead trees.

An aerial view of the canal along the east bank of the Broad and Congaree Rivers, from the South Carolina Electric & Gas Co. diversion dam on the Broad River to the Southern Railway Bridge on the Congaree River.

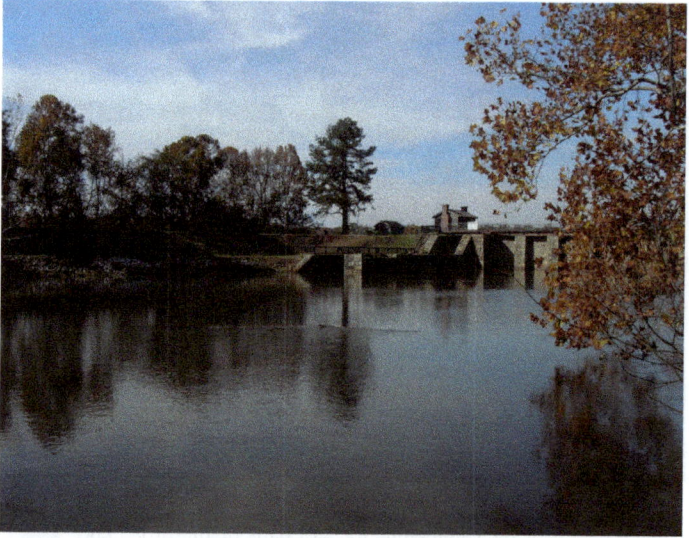

In 1815, the construction of a system of canals, sluices and locks began at Columbia on the Congaree, and above Columbia on the Broad and Saluda Rivers. The Columbia Canal was completed in January 1824, and the locks and sluices higher up on the Saluda River were completed in 1825. Some 45,612 bales of cotton were shipped through this waterway in 1827 and 48,574 went through in 1829.

Canal gate.

A view of the lock at the start of the canal. The channel widens immediately below the lock and the deep water runs swiftly.

A view of the Broad River Dam from the east. In 1836, a fifteen-hundred-foot dam was constructed in the Broad River near the confluence with the Saluda River to connect the Columbia Canal, which went around the fall line rapids.

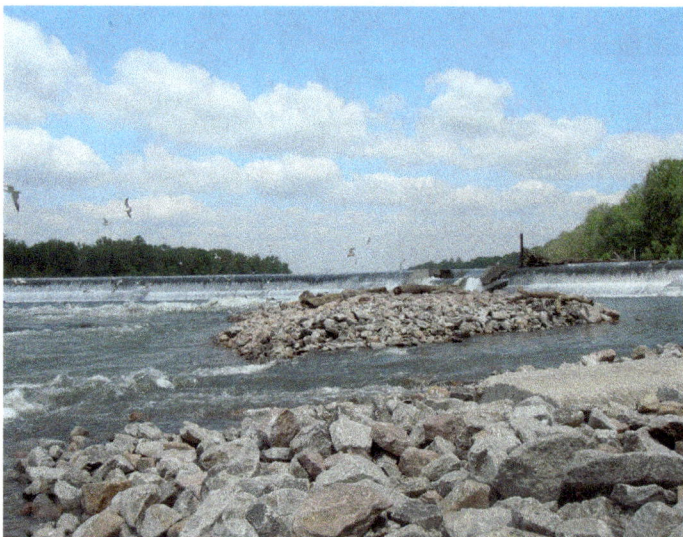

A view down the embankment of the dam.

Waterfalls on the Broad River.

The dam at the headwaters of the power canal.

The fall zone—rapids occur when the streams make a sudden descent.

The Broad River.

A Broad River waterfall.

A freight train crosses the trestle over the canal and the Broad River.

Mistletoe.

A rushing river. As colonies expanded inland, the rivers from the Lowcountry provided transportation to the Midlands through the fall lines where shoals and rapids occurred.

The Harbison State Forest boat landing on the Broad River.

The Columbia Waterworks.

The Columbia Waterworks pumping station on the Columbia Canal. It supplied spring water, which was forced up by steam power.

Water spilling through the weir.

A view of the former Irwin Park on the canal. The park was the creation of John Irwin, a longtime chief engineer at the city waterworks.

Twilight over the canal.

The canal is like a calm reservoir running along the east bank of the Broad and Congaree Rivers.

A wall of the South Carolina State Penitentiary. The deep, forbidding water of the lonely canal was a determent to those prisoners who were looking to escape from the penitentiary.

A turtle family at the zoo.

The Columbia Canal Hydroelectric Plant furnished electricity to homes, businesses and manufacturing plants. It is the oldest functioning part of the South Carolina Electric & Gas power system. There is a spillway from the power plant at the Gervais Street end of the Columbia Canal.

The EdVenture Children's Museum behind the hydroelectric plant.

This page and opposite: The Columbia Canal Hydroelectric Plant.

A lamp on the Gervais Street Bridge.

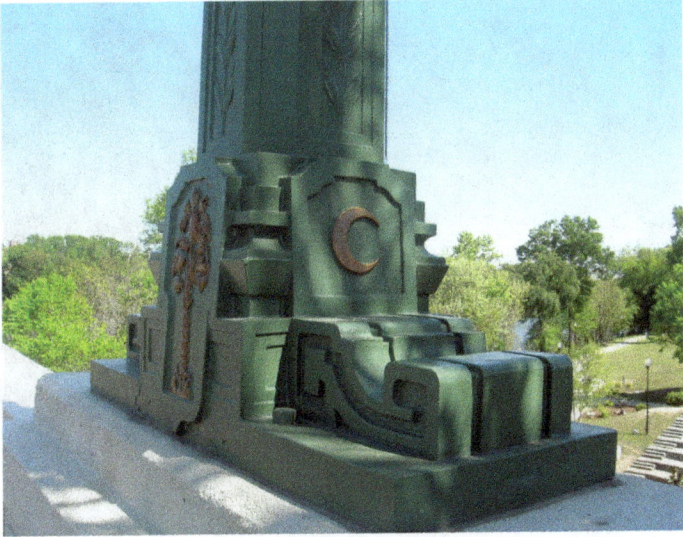

A detailed view of the lamp.

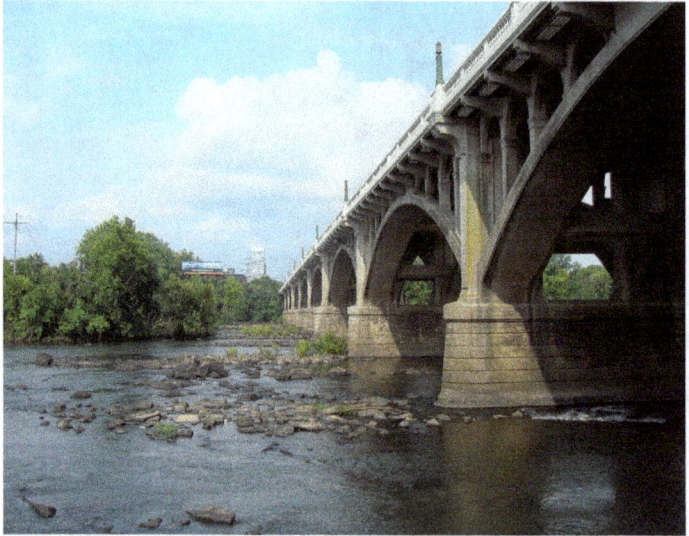

The Gervais Street Bridge leading to Columbia.

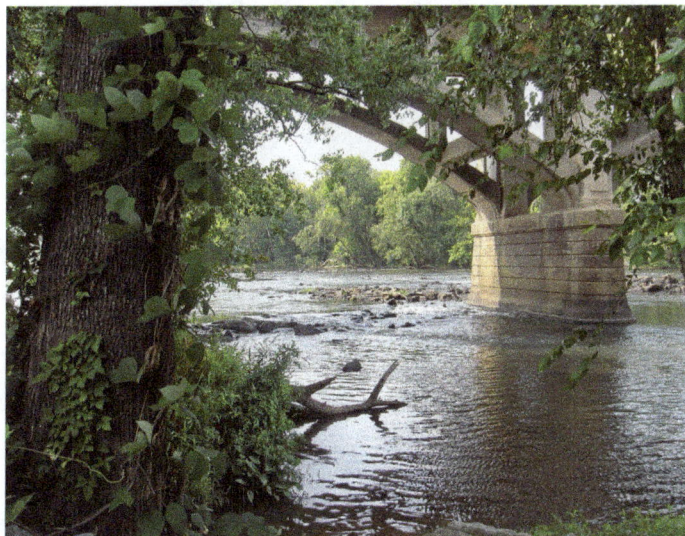

The view below the Gervais Street Bridge. It is important to pay attention to lights and sirens—when activated, leave the river immediately or make sure that you are prepared to deal safely with much higher and more forceful water flow.

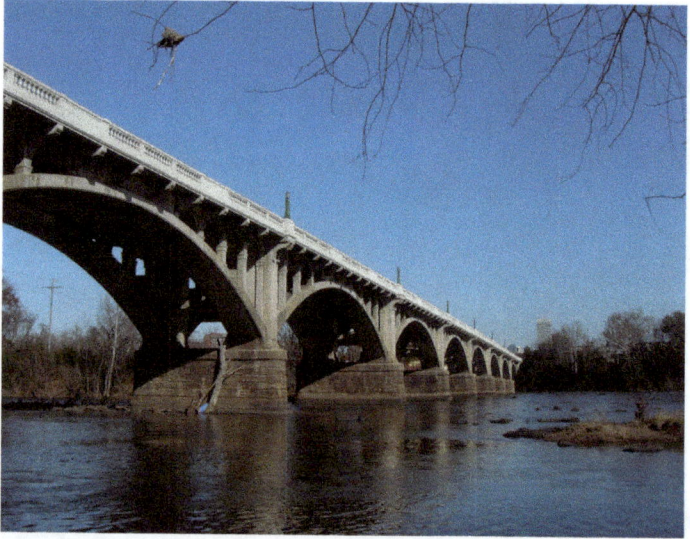

This page and opposite: Gervais Street Bridge.

Sherman threw shells onto the city from across the Congaree River on February 17, 1865.

The remains of a bridge burned to slow the entrance of Sherman and his army into the city of Columbia.

Twilight over the Gervais Street Bridge.

The McMillan Bridge at the end of Blossom Street handles traffic from the University of South Carolina.

The Jarvis Klapman Bridge.

The Columbia Canal served Columbia as an important route of transportation for about twenty years. After the arrival of the railroad in the decade from 1840 to 1850, it was practically abandoned.

A homeless shelter under the bridge.

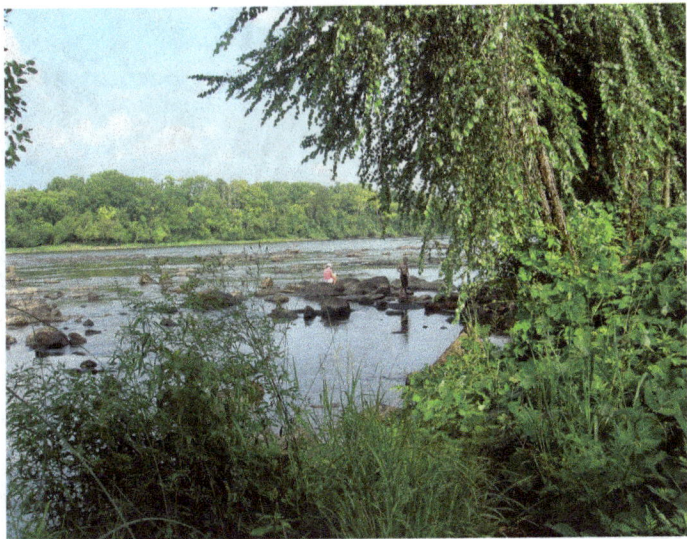

Reading on the rocks along the Congaree River.

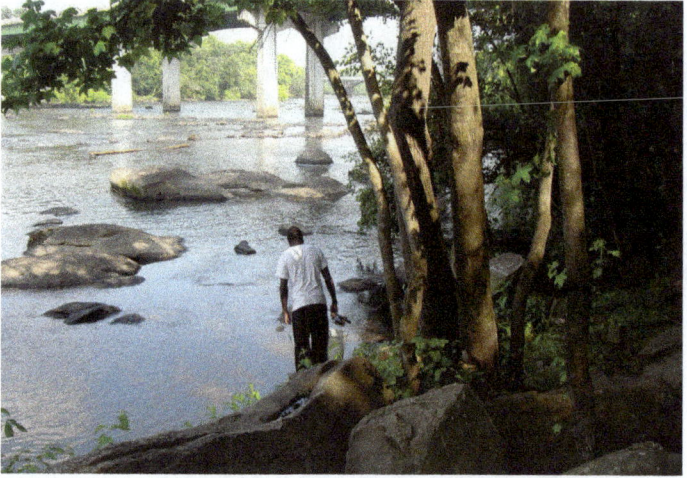

A man fishing near the Jarvis Klapman Bridge on the West Columbia side.

The Saluda River banks along West Columbia.

The Richland Distilling Company was built and put into operation in 1901 for the purpose of supplying liquor to the South Carolina Dispensary. After the abolition of the South Carolina Dispensary in 1907, the Richland Distilling Company went out of business and into bankruptcy.

The landing and locks below Cayce on the Congaree River.

The future site of an Innovista, University of South Carolina waterfront park and green space.

The Congaree River.

The Millrace rapids in the Saluda River near the zoo. The narrow shoreline with both slow and speedy currents and a natural fall line create a six-mile stretch of rapids.

Enjoying the Saluda River.

A Saluda lagoon.

Camping along the Saluda rapids.

The Riverbanks Zoo and Garden, one of America's top-rated zoos, is located along the Saluda River just one and a half miles from downtown Columbia. A footbridge crosses the river between the zoo and the gardens on the West Columbia side of the river.

The falls—or more correctly, the rapids—extend down the Saluda River. They make the river impassable except at flood stage, which creates open river conditions.

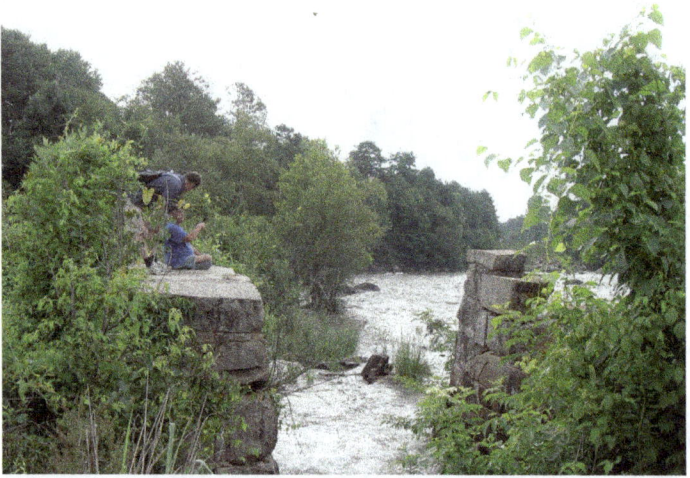

General Logan's corps crossed the Saluda River during the Civil War.
These are the remains of the Saluda Dam.

A race on the Saluda rapids.

The Vulcan Materials Company quarry. Historically, more than half of the aggregates it produces have been used in the construction and maintenance of highways, roads and streets and in other public works projects. The remainder has been used in the construction of housing, nonresidential buildings, commercial and industrial facilities, as railroad ballast and in nonconstructional uses, including agricultural and various industrial applications.

In 1856, a quarry was opened on the river where Granby Lane ran down to the landing where a ferry once operated. The statehouse was the first structure in the city made of stone from the quarry.

This page and opposite: Rhythm on the river.

Columbia, the first planned capital in America, was founded on March 26, 1786, and named for Christopher Columbus.

IRWIN PARK AT COLUMBIA WATER WORKS.

A postcard displaying Irwin Park at Columbia Waterworks. *Courtesy of the South Caroliniana Library, University of South Carolina.*

Sunset on the riverbanks. Columbia owes its existence to the fact that it was located at the head of navigation of three large rivers—the Broad, Saluda and Congaree.

Author photo by Caroline Jenkins.

Vennie Deas-Moore, author and local photographer, has published several books. Her books document people and their ties to the landscape. She is presently working as a visitor information specialist at the Columbia Regional Visitors Center. She has had twenty years of associations with the McKissick Museum at the University of South Carolina. Through her photographs and historical accounts of the rivers of Columbia, one can experience the waterways in a personal way.

The Columbia waterways are giving way to recreation and residential living. Though they are rapidly changing, Vennie has managed to capture and preserve in photographs a passing history of the riverbanks in Columbia, South Carolina.

Visit us at
www.historypress.net